ISBN-13: 978-1478179726
ISBN-10: 1478179724

The Publisher has strived to be as accurate and complete as possible in the
creation of this book.

This book is not intended for use as a source of legal, business, accounting
or financial advice. All readers are advised to seek services of competent
professionals in legal, business, accounting, and finance field.

In practical advice books, like anything else in life, there are no guarantees
of income made. Readers are cautioned to rely on their own judgment
about their individual circumstances to act accordingly.

While all attempts have been made to verify information provided in this
publication, the Publisher assumes no responsibility for errors, omissions,
or contrary interpretation of the subject matter herein. Any perceived
slights of specific persons, peoples, or organizations are unintentional.

For more information, please visit www.JackMize.com

Simple Online Reputation Management For Your Local Business

Table of Contents

Chapter 1

Your Online Reputation

 There is no such thing as privacy on the internet. Everything is searchable. There are more people looking for you online than you may think, and you can be sure that they'll find everything there is to be found about you.

This lack of privacy can range all the way from a Facebook "friend" becoming curious about you to government agencies and banks digging in to your past. The introduction of laws such as SOPA (Stop Online Piracy Act) and PIPA (Protect IP Act) created a huge and passionate debate because of the potential to compromise an individual's privacy rights.

The truth is, the internet has become such an interwoven part of our lives that it's time to take control and decide exactly what you want to reveal to the world – and what you want to keep private.

Whether you have noticed this yet or not, it has probably affected your business reputation as well. You just can't afford to ignore your business's online reputation. You have two choices:

1. Proactively manage and build your online reputation.
2. Reactively let others decide your online reputation.

If you chose the latter, the results could be disastrous.

So, you're asking yourself... "Why should I pay attention to online reputation management? I have a local business? It's not an *online* business, so, why does it matter? Yes, I have a website, but I haven't done anything *shady* online."

Like it or not, there's probably more information about you (and your business) online than you might imagine! But is it the right information? What story does it tell about your business? There are hazards, opportunities and, most importantly, strategies that allow you to exercise control over what potential customers find.

By educating yourself, you can better protect your business. You'll know what to do, whether you want to prevent or perhaps repair a bruised online reputation or, even better create a golden reputation that your prospects can easily find.

Why You Need to Manage Your Online Reputation

For the purposes of this discussion we will separate Reputation Management into three different phases. Keep in mind that your business can actually be moving through more than one of these phases at the same time:

- Building: In this phase you focus on building your online reputation if your business is just getting started or you may not have easily findable information about your great products or services. It includes creating a good reputation and maintaining it for your business.

- Maintenance: Once your business has built a good online reputation, that good image in the public's eye needs to be maintained. This can be an incredibly powerful, but often neglected phase.

- Recovery: If your business has elements of a bad reputation for any reason, then the recovery portion of reputation management is absolutely mandatory. You can't just throw up your hands. You can do something about it; in fact, you must do something about it because it will cost you customers and possibly your business.

Chapter 2

Who Is Checking You Out?

Let's face it; your potential clients are going to check up on you. Not only to see if you're trustworthy, but they want to know whether or not your ethics and business practices fit what they expect and need. They're looking for someone like them, someone they can identify with and someone they can trust.

Not only are your potential clients going to check up on you, but so are vendors, banks and anyone else that will be doing business with you. They want to know whether or not you have a bad payment history and if you deliver what you promise. They will be searching to see if there are complaints about you.

In short, what you say and do – online as well as offline – matters more than you might even realize. While there is no need for paranoia, there is definitely a need for caution – and even greater need to slow down and take stock of what information can be found about you and your business online.

The internet has made it easier and faster than ever for consumers, vendors and partners to perform a simple due diligence check on you. Will they find what you want them to find? Will what they find even be true?

Just "Google" It!

Think about it: It has become part of our culture to "Google" everything. You hear a song on the radio and want to find information about the band – you Google it. A family member tells you about a great new product – you Google it. Your best friend argues with you about who played guitar in that One Hit Wonder band from high school – you Google it.

You can count on current and prospective clients as well as potential (and existing) vendors, partners and financial backers Googling you!

And sometimes the only reason is

.... Curiosity

You may not be too worried about old friends searching for you on the internet (especially if your name is John Smith), but what about prospective clients, customers or vendors? What do they look for?

Search Engines: Weapons or Friends?

Today's search engines are becoming more and more powerful. Digging deeper is becoming easier.

For example, if you've had some recent achievement and your local paper is about to publish an article on you, what do you think the journalist writing it is going to do first?

That's right. She's going to Google you.

Well, get ready... because you do have some control over what she might find.

Chapter 3

What Will They Find?

Part of being proactive about your online reputation management is knowing what people will find when they look you up online.

Client Searches

There's a good chance that prospects who want to give you work are going to look for evidence that you can – or can't – be depended upon. Some of them will just Google your business name, others may add terms to their search like:

- Complaints
- Reviews
- Rip off
- And just about any other word relating to your specific business type or niche

It's bad enough when your name appears in the search results beside an "iffy" online review.

If there is a real problem with past customer experiences, the first page of the major search engine results are likely to have multiple entries detailing these accounts.

What people say (real or rumored) can have a tremendous impact on your online reputation. This, in turn, can ultimately have just as big of impact on your offline business. The real eye-opener: neglecting or failing to monitor your own online reputation and let others control what is found online can be the fastest and easiest way to do more damage than by actually doing anything wrong.

With the same ease in which bad information can pop up on search results, positive results can also appear when you are proactive about managing your online reputation.

Setting Up Alerts

17

There are ways to monitor your online reputation on an ongoing basis. The easiest, most automatic way is to set a Google Alert to tell you whenever anyone posts anything containing your name on the internet.

To set a Google Alert, simply visit the Google Alert creation page www.google.com/alerts and enter your own first and last name (in quotes) as your alert criteria.

Set your options as follows:

Once you create your alert you will receive an email whenever Google Alerts finds new results for your search. It's that simple. There is no reason not to do this NOW.

Chapter 4

Building Your Online Reputation

The key to having a solid, honest and positive online reputation is management. That's why you shouldn't sit back and assume there's nothing damaging to be found. Even if there is no negative information, you would also be neglecting a golden opportunity to build your business's:

- Credibility and authority
- Trustworthiness
- Popularity

When faced with options many consumers turn to the internet and simply "Google" a business's name as their first and often times only effort in performing due diligence.

Remember, an internet presence isn't just about being found online. It's also about having prospects *pick you* from other options available.

How an Online Reputation is Created

Like it or not you have an online reputation. It may not be extensive. It could even be what you feel is neutral, having no negative or positive slant. If that's the case, you can be certain it won't stay that way for long.

Whenever your business is mentioned online, whether it's on a forum, review, blog comment, or social media post there is a very good chance it will be "indexed" by search engines like Google. Search engines crawl the entire internet day and night discovering new content that has been published.

That's why setting your Google Alerts is so important. It can email you shortly after information about your business appears in its search index.

This is why a breaking story can almost instantly be found when you "Google" the subject. So, all it takes is one person to mention your business name on a public website to have it show up when someone else "Googles" your business's name.

Since there probably aren't millions, thousands or even hundreds of other websites competing with your business name as a search term, there is a high probability that this simple comment can show up on the first page of a Google search for your business name.

This is why online reviews are so powerful. They can be a prominent and even the only information that shows up on a search for your business name. This may be surprising and perhaps even a bit worrisome. But as you'll learn shortly, it could also be a huge benefit if you are proactive in managing your online reputation.

So how do online reputations grow? Some of the most common ways are...

What Others Reveal About You

Social media networks like Facebook, Twitter, LinkedIn, Google+, and YouTube are the fastest growing and most popular places people are spending their time on the internet. Unlike the early days when the internet was a one way street where the tech savvy fed information to the public, social media is primarily public user created content.

Anyone and everyone can have their voice heard by millions of people regardless of how logical, valid, or wanted it is.

It is the virtual online water cooler, where news, rumors, opinions, reviews, recommendations and about anything else you can talk about can be found. Given the right spin and momentum any of it can spread like wildfire through the internet. This has been given the term "gone viral."

So when someone, and when I say someone, I mean ANYONE, types in your business name and posts about your business on a social media network, whether it's good bad or indifferent, your online reputation has just been altered.

What You Reveal About Yourself

You may know your way around the web quite well. You've set up your social networking profiles, started your blog, have a customer friendly website. However, we must realize that as humans we simply don't spend every minute of every day focusing on potential online missteps. A simple conversation around something you are passionate about can sometimes carry us away. Sometimes it's just plain not knowing who can see what we are saying and we end up revealing more about ourselves to more people without being aware.

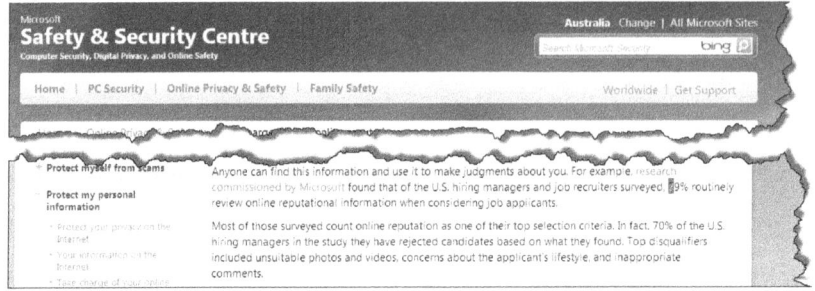

Realizing this fact should bring caution to mind. Statistics show that potential business partners, customers and clients will visit your social network pages and sites. They will Google your name.

You may think you're posting in private when you discuss your health problem on a dedicated forum – but that's not always the case. Many of the posts and responses you make are searchable, which in turn makes your comment findable by your prospects.

- You may think you're talking only to your friends when you share a quirky comment or let off steam – but then your friend (whose profile is public) re-posts your comment or quotes it.

- You may have forgotten all about that infamous hunt camp photo – but there it is: Your "friend" at work decides to post it to your wall, reminding you about it.

And that doesn't even begin to include the details we routinely reveal about ourselves in the course of enjoyable, informal chatting – comments that may not even represent the real you...

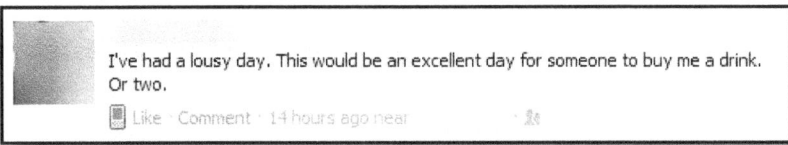

I've had a lousy day. This would be an excellent day for someone to buy me a drink. Or two.

Like · Comment · 14 hours ago near

You don't have to become a social media hermit. Just be careful and think before you post. The easiest thing for you to do is keep your personal social media identity separate from your business's social media identity.

Take advantage of the options for businesses on platforms like Facebook and Google+. Setup business pages and keep them focused on your business. Use your personal profiles to be social with online friends and family.

Chapter 5

The Good, The Bad & The Ugly

Let's start with the Good. One of the most powerful features of social media is that when you provide great products, services or customer experiences, your customers can share that with the world. This is your chance to take advantage of what 10 years ago might have been a little note of appreciation from a customer regarding their experience, to now allowing that customer to become an evangelist for your brand.

Instead of just letting you and maybe a couple of friends know, they can now instantly and directly notify hundreds or even thousands of virtually connected friends about how great you are and indirectly share their good news to millions of internet users because their comment has been picked up by the search engines.

Review and rating sites have become very popular. In the same way that social media posts are indexed, review and rating sites can and will show up when your business is "Googled." In fact, Google itself allows consumers to leave reviews right on your Google Local Business listing. So when your customers receive your great product or service they have an easy way to let the world know almost instantly.

Everyone's A Critic...

Ok, so now onto the Bad. I think you can see where this is going. For every advantage that you have for your customers to spread the good news about your business, there is an equal and opposite disadvantage if you fall short.

Unfortunately people are more likely to take action and talk about you when they feel they've been wronged in some way. However, you can change that with some simple strategies that we will go over later.

Many review sites give you, the business owner, a facility to respond to reviews or complaints. It's important that you do it in a constructive and non-argumentative fashion. Because you are not just responding the reviewer, you are also providing an impression of your business to all the viewers of that review and response.

If you are proactively managing your online reputation there is a good chance that happy customers will come to your defense, which is far more powerful than you arguing with the reviewer.

OK, I've Really Made Them Mad!

And now the ugly. You may find yourself on the wrong end of someone that is beyond irritated with your product or service, and they are truly angry and out for revenge. If a customer feels that they have been wronged or suffered real damage by doing business with you then they may take it as a personal mission to damage your business in return.

Now this is generally the exception, but given how easy it is to spread a message, it is something to treat as a real possibility and be prepared to defend your reputation.

What If It Isn't True?

You must also consider the disgruntled employee, the desperate competitor, the neighbor that you have a personal dispute with that just wants to get their jabs in anyway they can.

If someone is really angry with you, they may even set up a site dedicated to bad-mouthing you. Sure, you can have the site shut down if the attack is untrue or libelous ... provided you find out about it. But the trouble with wildfire is that even if you've stamped out one patch, another can easily burst into flame. The sad (and scary) part is ... without being proactive about monitoring your online reputation you won't even know others are watching you burn as you go about your business.

People may quote things you've said – things that you'd much rather they didn't and don't even remember saying (or even things you didn't say). They may tell derogatory stories about you – and let's face it, the stories worth repeating are never stories where you behave rationally and make no waves. The "best" stories are the "great big SPLASH" ones.

Don't make the mistake of thinking Facebook is the only place where these things happen: People may vent about you in their blogs. Worse, they may misunderstand something about you and make an earnest but absolutely inaccurate statement or comment about you – and it can show up almost anywhere.

You could find yourself talked about or quoted on social networks, blogs and in forum chatter – even though you, yourself, don't belong to these forums and barely visit Facebook.

This is why using a tool like Google Alerts is so important. It can be your second set of eyes to watch what is being said about you online 24 hours a day.

Chapter 6

Taking Control

You may be feeling thoroughly alarmed and overwhelmed, but there is good news.

Your simplest strategy is to take assessment of all the elements that make up your online reputation, good, bad and ugly. You have the opportunity to make the good even better, dilute and drown out the bad and the ugly by making sure all the "gold" shows up first and anything negative is so far back, even the pros won't get to it.

Having Defamatory Information Removed

While it can take some effort and commitment to have the bad and ugly buried, it can be extremely difficult to have it erased. You may ask "Why can't I simply ask the website owners for any derogatory information to just be removed?"

Well, you can and should, but go into it realizing that it is generally an uphill battle. Some the most common roadblocks are:

• The terms and policies of various platforms, like review sites and business directories are generally clear about the criteria required for data to be removed or changed, once entered. Most rest the burden on you, the business owner to prove that the information is inaccurate, and it falls within the realm of the impossible to prove that an opinion (review) is wrong.

- Many sites that your information appears on can be difficult to contact.

- Sometimes the site owners just don't want to remove the content and don't care about its accuracy.

- Even if you are successful in having the data removed, it may take months for search engines to update their indexed search results. So, even if the offending page is removed, the negative information can still show on the results page when someone "Googles" your business name.

If the information is copyrighted content that's original to you or comments about you that are genuinely defamatory and blatantly untrue, you absolutely should do your best to contact the site owner and request the offending information be removed immediately. Don't take a passive tone. If this is blatant you should demand action.

1. Start by sending a simple, direct statement that the information about you displayed on the website is either:

   a.   False

   b.   Unauthorized

2. Request that they remove the offending data immediately.

   - Keep it friendly but to the point stating the facts.
   - Being direct but non-hostile may avert an unpleasant situation.
   - Take the tone that you are simply informing them of the situation and you trust they will take action.
   - There is no need to explain the data or give a backstory.

3. If they refuse or provide no response in a reasonable time, contact them again. This time, make sure to include that this is a second request and you will have no option but to report them to their web hosting company within 48 hours if you don't receive a response or the data is not removed.

4. If they ignore this request, check their web host's site and read the rules and regulations.

5. Find a clause that applies to your case and constitutes a clear violation of their Terms of Service. Merely saying, "They've got lies about me on their website" won't cut it! You need to point out how the false or stolen material constitutes a direct and clear violation of a specific Term of Service.

6. Report the infraction to the web hosting company, quoting the exact violation.

Most web hosts have a lot to lose if one of their subscribers is posting content that could create an upstream legal accountability. If they take the site down it's amazing how a stubborn site owner's attitude and willingness to comply suddenly changes.

Finding Contact and Web Hosting information

Web Host information will not generally be found on the offending website. The easiest way to find who the webhost is would be to use Domain Tools, a free "whois" registry look-up service. You will immediately see at least the contact email address, phone and fax number supplied by the site owner.

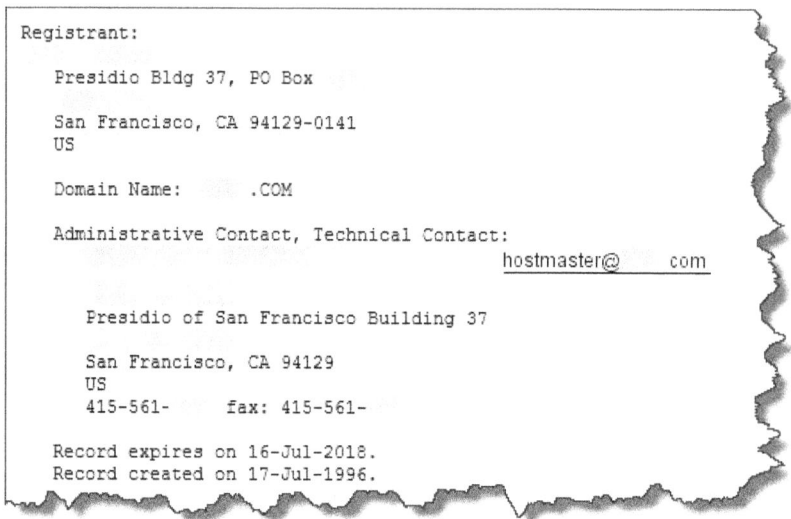

To find out who the site owners web-host is, simply select the *Server Stats* tab...

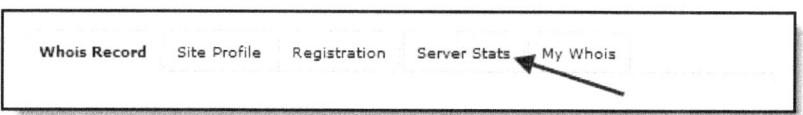

Their web hosting company will be displayed.

What If What They Are Saying Is True?

To be clear, this strategy is only likely to be effective if the information you want removed is false and libelous, or your copyrighted material.

If it's simply a negative opinion, review, accurate news piece or an embarrassing comment that you may have made without considering the consequences, you are unlikely to succeed in having it removed. A site owner may remove the data as a courtesy if you appeal on an emotional level. But you may not have any legal position to take.

Be careful before you act. Take careful consideration when reporting a site to their web host. When comments or stories are submitted to a website, it is considered voluntarily and with the poster's approval for it to be on display to search engines and members of the public across the world.

If you report a site because there is information or comments that you made that are merely embarrassing or ill-judged and it results in the web host taking that site offline, your actions could legally be considered malicious.

Removing Content from Google

Let's say that you were successful at getting a website to remove a negative piece of information. Even though they made the change, the negative result will still show up in Google for some time until they update their index.

If the negative item has been removed from the site and you need Google's index to reflect that immediately, you can go through Google's removal procedures to have that item taken out of the index. Here's how.

Start by going to the removal request page:

http://www.google.com/webmasters/tools/removals

Click "New Removal Request."

My Removal Requests

Use this page to request removal of a page or site from Google's search results.

Use this tool to remove content from Google search results.
You have no pending removal requests.

New removal request

Enter the URL you want removed.

New removal request

Enter the URL that you'd like to remove (case-sensitive)

Continue

Finally, select the reason you want it removed and hit the Request button.

Remove a URL from Google's search results

URL:

Reason:

Page has been removed or blocked from search engines	▼
Page has been removed or blocked from search engines	
The page has changed and Google's cached version is out of date	
The website owner won't remove personal content	
Inappropriate content appears in our SafeSearch filtered results	

There is no guarantee that Google will remove the info but it's worth going through these simple steps to try and expedite the removal of negative information.

Your Best Bet

If a website owner won't remove opinions, reviews, comments or any accurate information, regardless of how negative or embarrassing they may be, you still have powerful options.

Drown them out and push them further back with a good, solid batch of new and relevant search data!

Chapter 7

Make Things Happen

If you gotten this far you've most likely already "Googled" yourself and even setup your alerts. Well... what did you find? Good, bad or ugly? Perhaps, a little of each. Whatever you found, this is your starting point. So get let's get busy ...

Take Assessment

If you want to make sure your business makes a great first (page) impression, you need to evaluate what is currently found.

So, right now, Google the name of your business or your personal name if that's what prospects are more likely to search. The more unique the name the quicker and easier it will be to find the opportunities to tackle first.

To start with, let's do this with both your business name only then your business name and city, or local geographic area that a prospect would most likely look for. For example, "Acme Remodeling" and "Acme Remodeling Dallas, TX."

View the Results

The ideal results would include strong, positive information about your business such as:

- Your business's main website.
- Local business listings that include positive reviews
- Well-optimized social network profiles like LinkedIn, Facebook, Google+, etc.)
- Your expert positioning YouTube Video Channel and individual videos
- Relevant press releases about the positive effects your business has on your customers and local community.

If your results aren't exactly ideal, don't despair – you are going to improve them shortly. Meanwhile, dig through at least the first five pages and save every undesirable entry you find.

First, Change What You Can

Starting with:

- Business Listing information
- Social network profiles
- Contact site owners about unauthorized or false information you want removed.

How Long Does it Take?

Unfortunately you have little control over when the changes you make actually appear in the search results. However, if you focus on large high traffic sites that regularly show up on the front page of Google, you have a very good chance that your changes could appear in a few days and sometimes as little as a few hours.

To give yourself the highest expectation for success you should:

- Sign up for relevant social networks
- Register or claim your listing in local business directories
- Make sure your profiles are accurate and complete
- Create blog posts about your business
- Submit press releases
- Write some articles and submit them to article directories

Don't think of this as a painful chore – think of it as a chance to take control of your online reputation, expert positioning and brand.

Chapter 8

Making the Most of Social Media

Social Media networks carry a lot of authority with search engines like Google. So while getting your own website ranked high might seem like a huge task, having information about your business that sits on Social Media pages ranked on the first page can be very fast and easy to accomplish.

LinkedIn

LinkedIn can be an extremely powerful online networking tool for making business connections and building an expert reputation within the community. One of the greatest side benefits of a well optimized LinkedIn profile is the high probability of grabbing a first page spot in the search engines very quickly for your personal name and business name.

You can take this power even further by participating in discussions and encouraging your clients and vendors to provide recommendations within the LinkedIn community.

Recommendations on LinkedIn are usually genuine and have a higher value than a simple "Like" on Facebook.

Optimizing your LinkedIn information to give it a better chance to rank highly in Google search results for your name and business is pretty easy if you follow these twelve steps.

1. Fill out your profile as completely as possible. The more detail you provide about yourself and your business, the higher it should rank.

2. Keep in mind that your customers, prospects and vendors will be viewing your LinkedIn information when they see it in Google search results. Make sure the information you share is professional and relevant to the message that would be most compelling to your target rather than your achievements. Consider this a professional marketing opportunity instead of a resume.

3. Use your main keywords in your "Professional Headline" (LinkedIn Profile Heading). This may be a "What You Do" rather than "Who You Are" statement.

4. Repeat your "What You Do" statement in your "summary" – the text box that allows you to write a short paragraph about yourself. For example "At YOUR BUSINESS NAME we HELP...."

5. Include your main website URLs to your profile (this includes other social network pages that can strengthen your good online reputation).

6. Add valuable connections and join relevant groups. Make sure you keep your target customers, prospects and vendors in mind.

7. Be sure and ask for valuable recommendations. It's not unusual or considered bad etiquette to solicit recommendations on LinkedIn from people you've worked with, and don't be stingy when others ask for recommendations from you if they've provided value.

8. Update your status weekly at the very least.

9. Make sure your profile is set to "Public!" No one will be able to find you if you neglect this simple but crucial step.

Customize Your Public Profile

Control how you appear when people search for you on Google, Yahoo!, Bing, etc.

Profile Content
- Make my public profile visible to **no one**
- Make my public profile visible to **everyone**

10. Create a custom LinkedIn URL with your name, if available. To do this, go to

    a. "Settings" menu

b.   Select "Edit your Public Profile"

c.   Select "Customize Your Public Profile URL" in the blue "Your Public Profile URL" box (bottom right of that page):

Your public profile URL

Your current URL

http://ca.linkedin.com/in/
Customize your public profile URL • View your public profile

Note that you can also "View your Public Profile" – the way others see it – on this tab.

11.   Create a profile badge – and share your LinkedIn URL across your other social network profiles, pages and websites. (You'll find the link to this function in the box right below "Your public profile URL".)

Profile Badges

Create a profile badge to promote your profile like this:

View my profile on **Linked** [in]

---

12.   Upload a professional photo of yourself.

Jack Mize (3rd)

Local Internet Marketing and Mobile Marketing Expert at JackMize.com

Houston, Texas Area   Marketing and Advertising

Use the same image across all your profiles for a consistent brand.

Facebook

If you already have a Facebook account, login as soon as possible, right now even, and optimize all of your Account and Privacy settings. Delete anything you don't want to show up in search results – and make sure each individual setting or section is made either public or private, depending on what you want the world to see.

Regularly check those settings – Facebook has an annoying habit of changing their default settings to Public on occasion.

Facebook SEO fundamentals are similar to LinkedIn's – with one major bonus... You can create a free Facebook Page for your business! This is separate from your personal profile; however, your personal profile is needed to actually create and manage the Facebook Page.

Keep this page updated and focused around your business rather than personal posts. As a professional courtesy acknowledge comments by others by "Liking" their post.

For a quick cleanup of your past, login and look under "General Account Settings," click "Download a copy of your Facebook data" to download all your past posts. It's an easy way to see which posts you'd like to permanently remove.

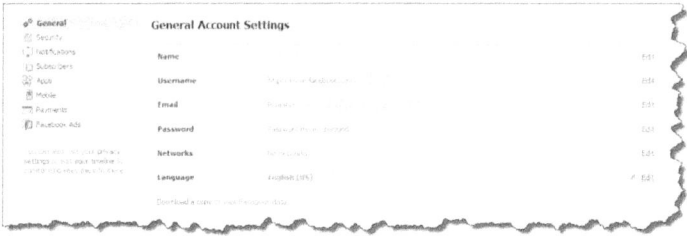

If you don't want your email address to be visible to Friends, you also need to specify this under your "Account Settings" tab. Facebook recently changed your default email address to your Facebook assigned @facebook.com, so be sure and adjust that if it's not the email you want to use.

Finally, as with LinkedIn, be sure to create a "Like" badge and share it across all your business related social networking profiles and websites.

Twitter

Follow the same tips for Twitter. Write your bio with your customers, prospects and vendors in mind. Keep it professional, because all your tweets will probably turn up in search engine results! This is also true with the photos you share. So if it's information that can have positive impact on your reputation make sure your business name is clearly in the message.

You can also create a badge for twitter to post your other business sites – so people can share your site content. This can also increase your social network rankings.

YouTube

Creating a YouTube Channel for yourself (using your full name and business name where available) can be one of the most effective ways to build your good reputation.

Don't worry about making polished, professionally produced videos. It is unnecessary and can sometimes work against you.

The key is to focus on content. Make a short video – less than 3 minutes, giving a very specific and valuable message to your target audience. This should not be an advertisement or an "all about me" video. This video should position you as an educator and an advocate for the success of your customers' and prospects' success.

By doing this you don't have to call yourself the expert. Your viewers will attach that title to you in their minds, which is far more valuable.

YouTube videos have an extremely high probability of showing up on the first page of Google very quickly. To apply this directly to your online reputation you should make sure your business name is in the Title of the video. You also want to put the full URL of your main website as the very first line of the video's description (http://yourwebsite.com) this can greatly increase your search engine ranking – as well as help brand your business, and create your "expert" status.

If you have the opportunity to get happy customers and clients to go on camera and talk about what a great experience they had doing business with you, do it! This is one of the most credible and powerful social proofs for your Online Reputation.

Google+

Google's own social network has been described as "Facebook meets LinkedIn" and appears to combine the best features of both – with a very strong Local orientation. This makes it a powerful tool for your online business reputation if optimized correctly. Similarly to Facebook, Google+ allows you to create business pages within the network.

One of the greatest benefits is that Google has now merged its very powerful and local market specific Google Places listings into the Google+. This brings not only your business name, description, location, contact info and customers reviews to the front page, but also the compelling messages you create on your Google+ Business Page.

Here are four essential tips for a brand-building page that can build your expert status...

1.   Make sure you invite only quality people to your Circles. (They'll display on your Google+ Page)
2.   Make sure you join only Circles relevant to your business and branding
3.   Have your keywords (what you do) in your headline/tagline
4.   Create a badge – and use it on your sites!

Reputation Boosters

Social networks can be strong reputation boosters.

•   Always keep in mind your target customers, prospects and vendors.

- Avoid social networks that you feel don't fit your business – they'll waste time you could better spend elsewhere.

Get to know the most active demographic group for each major social network... and concentrate your efforts to only those suiting the specific target audience for your business.

If you're not sure where to start, for the purpose of reputation building, I'll suggest the following order.

1. LinkedIn
2. Facebook
3. Google+
4. YouTube
5. Twitter

Chapter 9

Online Directories & Review Sites

Social networks are not the only quality sites with high rankings. In fact, online business directories based on geo-targeted locations can create a fast and high impact presence on the front page of the search results for your business name.

Several of these sites have already created a basic listing for your business based on information they have pulled from other sources like the Yellow Pages, local phone company and other aggregators of business information. For this one reason you should make sure that your information is correct on as many sites as possible since it may actually "sync" with other sites and directories across the Internet.

Most of the sites that have already created your business listing give you, the business owner, an opportunity to "claim" and edit the information of your basic listing for free. It is very important that you do this and is usually as simple and filling out some information online that will allow them to verify you are indeed the owner or agent for the business.

Most of these sites have a section that says something like: "Is this you? Claim your listing now." Click on the button and verify your information – correct any mistakes or outdated information, while completing as much information as possible in your profile.

A quick trick to finding sites that have already established a basic listing for your business is to enter "claim business listing YOUR BUSINESS NAME" into a Google search. This should bring up a list of sites that contain your business name with an option to claim a listing.

Below are some of the most popular business listing sites on which you may want to claim or create your business listing.

Google+ Local

This is part of your Google+ Profile (formerly Google Places, and before that Google Maps).

Angie's List

Angieslist.com is a U.S.-based "word-of-mouth" online referral service that is considered a solid authority site. You can sign up, or simply join through your Facebook or Google log in.

"Ordinary" consumer members are encouraged to refer local businesses that have provided excellent service. Recommendations cannot be bought and are considered 100% authentic.

Having happy customers recommend you on Angie's List can create instant credibility and a great way to build on your golden online reputation.

Yelp!

Yelp.com is local business referral and review site has been considered one of the top places that consumers go to leave and check reviews for local businesses.

You can "claim" your listing... or you can pay for a "premium" listing (which can, ironically, have less value to some consumers because they don't see it as organic feedback from others).

It's a good idea to claim or create a listing for your business and encourage your happy customers to leave reviews.

Merchant Circle

MerchantCircle.com is one of the true gems for local businesses when it comes to being found on Google. Not only do Merchant Circle business listings frequently show up on the front page of Google, there are also features such as coupons, connections to other businesses and a blogging platform that allows you to post several articles and information to better position yourself as the expert.

You can claim and optimize your Merchant Circle listing for free. There are several opportunities to upgrade to a paid listing but it is unnecessary for our initial purposes.

Getting Good Local Reviews

Make sure all information you provide online sites about your business is:

- Accurate
- Descriptive
- Focused on the benefits of doing business with you

Let prospects know what to expect when doing business with you.

Always set out to deliver exactly what you promise. The phrase "over deliver" is used quite a bit, but the fact is if you simply deliver what you promise, you'll beat your competition hands down.

Don't underestimate consistency. The most successful fast food national service franchises, and just about any other type of business that has customers coming back again and again, have one thing in common: Consistency. They may not have the best product or service, but if customers get what they expect it can rate higher than just about any other quality (think McDonalds).

Chapter 10

Reviews and Comments

Handling Bad Reviews and Comments

Odds are if you have been in business for a while there has been an unhappy customer, disgruntled employee, or someone that feels the need to throw a snag in your business by posting something negative about your business.

Here's how to handle it:

1.   Delete any spam

2.   If anything is libelous or blatantly untrue, check the site policies; then notify the directory owner or administrator with specific details about the post. Feel free to dispute it yourself, if you are able to – but do make sure you provide empirical and undisputable proof (e.g. "I'm sorry to hear you had such a bad experience, but you seem to be confusing us with Acme Plumbing in Eugene, Oregon. My business is "Acme Plumbing Supply" based in Texas. I'm afraid we don't serve your area or offer repair services!")

3.   If a bad review is accurate, don't just pretend it doesn't exist and hope it will go away. Contact the reviewer and address their complaints. Take responsibility and offer a solution to their

problem. If you can successfully resolve their problem it is absolutely acceptable to ask that the review or post be removed or amended.

4. Learn from the experience. Sometimes a bad review is really a wake up call to a problem in your business that you might not know exists. Take this opportunity to fix what is broken.

Getting Great Reviews

First – ask! Ask on your website, on your menu, business card, or social network business pages. "Like our food? Leave a review at [www.directoryURL.com]." Drop hints by writing things like "Your referral is the best thanks we can get" at the bottom of your invoices.

Ask on your Facebook and Google+ Page. "Leave a comment or review if you love us!"

Testimonials from happy customers can be a very effective way to build a strong reputation online. They provide social proof that your product or service is great. Video testimonials can be one of the most powerful pieces of online real estate you can have. They don't need to be polished. Just a simple statement from a happy customer recorded with a flip camera or smartphone will do the trick.

If appropriate for your business, especially with large transactions, ask customers to fill out a short survey, which includes permission to share their comments with others.

Chapter 11

Power of Press Releases

Press releases are not just for big companies breaking big news. Chances are your business has press release worthy activity on a weekly basis.

The great thing about press releases is they can spread quickly to multiple sites on the internet, even to the websites of major news outlets like TV networks, local newspapers and magazines.

Now your story might not be a front-page feature, but just having your press release buried deep inside one of these authority sites does the trick.

When someone "Googles" your business name and your press release is displayed on the local FOX, NBC, CBS news website, it adds instant credibility.

Your simple press release being picked up and distributed to theses sources will allow you to ethically display "As Seen On...." followed by the national brand.

What Should My Press Release Be About?

Your press release should not be a blatant advertisement about your business. To create a press release that has a high chance of being picked up by news outlets you should tie something about your business, like a new product release, or store opening, even how a customer successfully used your product or service, to a current event.

Remember that this should be the facts and no hype, so keep adjectives like "incredible, FREE, amazing" out of the story. Don't forget the old news formula and include the who, what, where, when, why and how of the story.

Most press release distribution services have great example templates and best practices to follow for a successful press release. Here are some press release distribution services you can check out.

Prweb.com
BusinessWire.com
EReleases.com

The goal of your press release is to position your business as the place to get quality and expert services without looking like a blatant advertisement

Chapter 12

Outsourcing Your Online Reputation Management

By now you realize how important it is to monitor, maintain and create your business's good online reputation. You may also think "Whew, that's a lot of stuff to keep up with." You should consider outsourcing to a professional online reputation management or internet marketing company that specializes in helping local businesses.

The advantage of a using a professional really depends on their specialized knowledge of the areas we discussed. Make sure they can navigate the twists and tricks to making sure your business is well positioned, and not being damaged by anything on the net. It is especially important that they are well versed in the needs of local businesses and habits of local consumers.

There are knowledgeable consultants with fair prices and options out there. Ask for examples of their work with local businesses and then, well, go "Google" them.

Conclusion

Building a Golden Reputation is simply getting into the habit of checking your name in top search engines at least once a month. Make part of your schedule, put it on your calendar and follow through.

Getting into the habit of monitoring and maintaining your online reputation is your best course of action against any embarrassing "mentions" that may crop up. It can also help you get more prospects to "pick you" when they have multiple options. Even if there isn't anything bad about your business, having some golden content out there may be what tips them in your favor.

Ask yourself:

- Who am I?
- What do I want my target audience to see?
- Is this something I'll be proud of having associated with me and my business?

Keep those questions in mind every time you post anything on the web and you'll be well on your way to creating a powerful internet persona, sterling reputation and just maybe branded as a local subject matter expert or celebrity in your field.

About The Author

Jack Mize is a Local Internet Marketing expert and small business consultant who helps businesses get more customers by making their compelling message "findable" online.

Jack's focus on the search and buying behavior of consumers when they are looking to buy locally led him to develop his method of opening "Lead Valves." This strategy allows local businesses to be found in multiple places with a message that converts searchers into prospects and prospects into customers.

By identifying problems that local consumers need to solve locally and creating "Lead Valves" that provide the solution, Jack has developed a system that is laser focused on the quality of the conversion rather than the quantity of internet traffic.

In 2009 Jack began teaching his Lead Valve strategy to Local Internet Marketing consultants and small business owners around the world.

By teaching his students how to reposition themselves from traditional hard sales tactics to being the educators and advocates for their clients success, Jack has been credited with saving businesses and changing lives.

To learn more about Jack Mize and receive up to date information on what's working in Local Internet Marketing by one of the leading experts, visit www.JackMize.com

www.ingramcontent.com/pod-product-compliance
Lightning Source LLC
Chambersburg PA
CBHW071618170526
45166CB00003B/1103